SUMMER OF FROGS

SUMMER OF FROGS

DAWN WHITE

Dawn Elaine-Gilbert White

Published by
Dawn Elaine-Gilbert White
P. O. Box 35
Rock Island, TN 38581

Cover art and design © Dawn Elaine-Gilbert White
Printed and bound in the United States

ISBN 978-0-578-79751-9

CONTENTS

ACKNOWLEDGEMENTS

Many thanks to my writing partner, friend, and mentor, Diane Tilton-Mauer, who has always been a gracious and willing editor of my stories.

Thank you to my loving and supportive family who know that when I'm writing, I'm lost in another world. Thanks for allowing me to visit that world when I need to.

Although this is a work of fiction, the story was inspired by my memory of finding myself alone at sixteen years old in the Caney Fork Gorge below the Great Falls Dam in Rock Island State Park as the sun was setting. When it gets dark out there, it gets very dark, very quickly.

To my childhood friends, thanks for the memories. To my parents and the rivers, mountains, and woods of Tennessee, thanks for helping me grow up.

CHAPTER 1

You'd think it was Thanksgiving, but it's just a regular dinner for the four of us that Mama's preparing for tonight. It's only two o'clock in the afternoon, but judging by her frenzy you'd think we were all about to starve to death. Gluttony is the only one of the seven deadly sins that church folk seem to ignore. Lust? Forget it. Sloth? No way. But food? Her life revolves around food. She's not overweight or anything. But she tries to stuff as much food as possible down the rest of us.

When Mama's done cleaning up the breakfast dishes she starts cooking lunch, when those dishes are sparkling, it's time to get going on dinner. She has a dishwasher, but I never see her use it. She polishes each dish and cup with her dishtowel. Same with her clothes dryer. She says hanging clothes out on the line is better. The sun and fresh air give them that clean smell you just can't get from the inside of a dark hunk of metal.

Mama scurries around the kitchen tending to three different saucepans on the stovetop, slowing down only to peek through the oven window. "I left a message for Miss Bertie asking her to drop off some of her *dee-licious* sourdough bread," she says.

"Do we have to have bread again tonight?" I say. "I don't need all those carbs, Mama."

"Trixie, Miss Bertie makes the *best* bread! How could you

1

turn down Miss Bertie's homemade bread? She's getting on up there. Who knows how much longer she'll be around to make that good sourdough."

Mama has a way of making everything sound like a commercial. She's always in on the secret recipe for everything in life, and you just *have* to try what she suggests or you'll really miss out.

I hop up on the wooden stool in Mama's kitchen. I used to like to sit here when I was little and watch her cook. I stopped asking if I could help a long time ago. Mama doesn't like anyone else messing around in her kitchen. Now that I'm sixteen, I don't sit on this stool so much anymore.

"You're too thin as it is, Trixie." Mama whisks by me in her green gingham apron on her way back to the oven. "You could use some of Miss Bertie's good sourdough bread."

"Gosh, Mama, is there anyone in the world you *don't* think is too thin?"

Mama's just starting to open the oven door when she stops and whirls around, a stained potholder in each hand. "Trixie, you know we don't say *gosh* in this family."

"Yes ma'am," I say.

I remember when my little sister said *fart* on the way to church one Sunday morning. I thought Mama was gonna wreck. She turned around and said, "What did you just say, Ruth Ann?"

"I *tooted*," Ruth Ann said.

"That's better," Mama said.

Daddy turned and winked at me. I was sitting behind Mama. If he could have done it without Mama seeing, I'm sure he would have turned all the way around and winked at Ruth Ann, too.

Even though Daddy's job is driving a big truck, Mama's always the one that drives the family. He told me one time, "It's just easier to let her do the driving, Little Bit. That way she doesn't have to keep telling me what all I'm doing wrong."

I think Daddy is happy, most of the time. I heard he sure was happy back when Mama agreed to marry him. She was Miss Bartow County, after all. And she was a runner-up for Miss Georgia.

"Can you go wake Ruth Ann up from her nap?" Mama says. "I need to listen for Miss Bertie. I wanna find out what happened at the church meeting last night. And I don't want Ruth Ann sleeping all afternoon, then she'll be up all night."

"Yes, ma'am," I say, sliding off the stool. I'm ready to go call Grace anyway. It's the perfect time of day for us to work on our tans. I love summer. Grace has lived down the street from me since we were six years old, and every summer since has been *our* summer.

I open Ruth Ann's bedroom door. She looks so cute lying there all spooned up with her stuffed rabbit, her blond hair damp with perspiration. She always gets hot when she sleeps, even when it's *not* ninety degrees outside.

"Buttercup?" I sit on the edge of her bed and touch her flushed cheek. "Wake up, darlin'."

She doesn't move. I watch her sleep for a few minutes. Her eyelids haven't lost that translucent look from when she was a newborn. I love it how babies sleep that death sleep, where nothing in the world could wake them from that sweet dream they're having.

I'm thirteen years older than Ruth Ann. She's Mama's late-in-life child. The one they tried for years to have. When they finally gave up and reconciled themselves to the fact that I would forever be an only child, Ruth Ann decided to enter this world and grace us with her charming presence. She's Mama's favorite. For one thing, she looks just like Mama. They're both small, with creamy skin, faded blue eyes, and fine, yellow-blond hair. I look like Daddy. We're tall, with dark hair and olive skin.

I think Ruth Ann came just in time. It was at a point in Mama's life when she was starting to lose her zip. She wasn't walking around the house singing anymore. She sat in the easy chair with her Bible open in her lap, staring out the sliding glass doors into the trees. Daddy said it was probably *the change* coming on, but as soon as she found out she was expecting, she was her old self again. And then Ruth Ann came along and looked just like her, mannerisms and all. Mama seemed to get ten years back on her life.

I don't mind that Mama is so crazy about Ruth Ann. Shoot, who wouldn't be crazy about that kid? She has this look behind her eyes like she's much older than her years. Like she has things figured out. Like just by being around her you'll learn things, find the answers to what's been bugging you. She's not one of those whiny, bratty kids I see at the mall. Ruth Ann is special.

"Wake up, Buttercup," I say, rubbing her back.

Her eyelids flutter, then she tries to focus on me. "Hi, Sissy. Is it morning?"

"Nope. You just took a nap. It's still the same day. Why don't you get up so you can go out and play?"

"Okay," she says, wiping the sleep out of her eyes.

I kiss her head then walk into my room and pick up the phone. I dial the number I've had memorized since before I could read and write.

"Moon Turkey," I say, "meet me at the speed limit, okay? Bring your baby oil. I've got the lemon juice."

Grace's been *Moon Turkey* and I've been *Red Feather* for the past couple of years, ever since our Tom and Huck adventure down the river that runs by both our houses. We took one of those flimsy little inflatable boats, no bigger than an inner tube, and decided to launch it from our neighbor's dock. We had to criss-cross over each other so we'd fit. Our four long legs dangled in the water, but somehow we managed to push off. Though there was a swift current, we paddled with the two tiny plastic oars about a mile down the river, then scrambled to get over to a dock before we got any closer to the waterfall down by the bridge.

I slip into my two-piece—the most decent one Mama and I could find, only allowed for sunbathing in the backyard, not for mixed swimming— and head down the road to meet my friend and walk her back to my house.

When we were little and just *had* to see each other, our mamas would let us meet at the bent-up speed limit sign by the road that's halfway in between our houses. When I got close enough to read, "30 m.p.h.," I knew I was almost there. Grace and I would hang out at that sign until one of us finally got called home. It was usually Mama calling me with her trademark two-tone whistle, more dignified and far-reaching than Mrs. Barnes' shout.

I'm carrying my sandals with the straps looped over my finger. The asphalt is hot, but I don't wanna put on my shoes. At the beginning of every summer I have to get my feet toughened up and used to being bare again. I look up and see Grace waving madly. Just the sight of her warms me. When we're alone, away from school, we act much younger than our sixteen years. I start skipping, then Grace starts skipping. When we finally reach each other, Grace throws down her bottle of baby oil, and we fall into our hand-slap routine. It begins with us slapping our own legs, then each other's hands in the air, and after twisting and turning, slapping and clapping from all different angles, we drop to the ground, sitting back to back, and then stand while pushing against each other. It ends with a handshake as our free hands point at each other, then we freeze. No one else knows the routine but us.

On my back patio, we slather on the baby oil, doing each other's backs. We wet our hair with the garden hose and rub lemon juice into it. We lie on towels in the lounge chairs and wait for the summer sun to kiss our skin and hair. We don't need to talk.

CHAPTER 2

As the sun starts to dip behind the mountains, Grace says, "I gotta run home. Call me later."

I wander back inside, my skin warm and flushed. Mama and Miss Bertie are sitting in the parlor. It's the room with the nicest furniture in the house. We don't use it, it's just where Mama seats guests who come to the front door. They hush their voices when I enter the room.

Mama looks up at me. "Yes, Trix? Did you need something?"

"I just wondered what time we're having dinner," I say. Miss Bertie's eyes move up and down as she takes inventory of my two-piece.

Mama must have noticed Miss Bertie's eyes because she says, "Why don't you go put something on, Honey? Dinner will be at six o'clock."

Then she says to Miss Bertie, as if I'm not still standing there, "She only wears that silly thing in the backyard—got this crazy notion about needing a tan—for what reason I'll never know!"

Miss Bertie sniffs at her cup of tea then takes a sip.

"Can Grace spend the night?" I say. Mama will never say no in front of company.

"Of course," she says, then she lets out that nervous chuckle of hers and shakes her head at Miss Bertie as if to say, *Kids these days*. But Miss Bertie doesn't even smile. She looks like she's about a hundred, face and body so wrinkled and droopy I can't begin to tell what she must have looked like before. Her hair is dyed pitch black. And she always wears a plain dress, nothing patterned or colorful. In fact, she must have been born ancient. She looks exactly the same as she did when I was a little kid and first saw her at church.

As far as I'm concerned, Miss Bertie *is* the First Baptist Church. When my family started going there, we quickly learned that Miss Bertie knew everything about everybody in the flock. If someone went forward on Sunday in need of prayer, by the next day Miss Bertie had found out what their secret sin had been and promptly started the gossip chain. I mean, the prayer chain.

I know today Mama has been getting an earful of the most recent transgressions. I don't know why either one of them is so interested in other people's business. And I wish Mama didn't care so much what people think about her.

As I turn and strut out of the parlor, I smile to myself, thinking how my two-piece will be Miss Bertie's next phone call.

"I'm not one to bear false witness against my neighbor," she'll say. Then pressing her thin lips against the mouthpiece, she'll lower her crackly voice. "*But . . .*"

CHAPTER 3

Grace and I sneak into the kitchen around midnight, scrounging for snacks. After picking at Mama's casserole, and getting her all flustered, I'm just now finally starting to feel hungry. I can't help it if I was still too stuffed from her ham and tomato sandwiches at lunch to eat an early dinner.

The house is dark and quiet as I feel my way to the kitchen with Grace hangin' onto my nightshirt from behind. Mama believes in *early to bed, early to rise*, so she and Daddy are already asleep. And, of course, Ruth Ann was tucked in hours ago. That kid sure sleeps a lot. Mama says Ruth Ann is delicate like a Georgia peach.

When my fingers find the light switch, I flip it on. "Why don't we get some jam and put it with *Miss Bertie's dee-licious sourdough bread*," I whisper, giggling at my imitation of Mama.

Grace covers her mouth with her hands to stifle her hiccup-y laugh. She knows she can get loud when she gets tickled, and everyone's bedroom is all in a row right down the hall.

On tiptoe, we carry two glasses of cold milk, napkins, and plates with the jam and bread back to my room with the help of the kitchen light I left on. Then I go back to turn the light off and make my way in the darkness alone. I know this house so well I can easily navigate it blind. Mama and Daddy lived here even before I was born, and they'll never move. For a second, I try to picture Mama in her kitchen, as old and creaky as Miss Bertie, but I can't imagine Mama letting herself get old. I can see Daddy, though, all bent over, whiskers growing out of his ears. But then I see the sliver of light under my bedroom door, and the picture disappears.

When Grace and I finish wiping our mouths clean we set our plates on the floor. We both know Mama will be pleased to see the empty plates in the morning. She never minds people eating in her house, even if it's in the middle of the night.

We lie back in bed and pull up our nightshirts to compare bloated bellies. I know every line of my friend's body, as she does mine. Over the years there were months she was taller than me, then I'd catch up. We finally leveled off with me beating her by a few inches.

"Do you think my hair looks blonder?" Grace says.

I pick up a strand of her sandy, shoulder-length hair and examine it. "I think so. You're lucky—you started out close to blond." I don't have to look to know my hair color hasn't changed one bit.

Grace crooks her right arm over her head against the pillow. "Remember that time we got out the tape measure to see whose boobs were bigger?"

"Weren't yours wider across and mine stuck out farther?"

"Something like that," Grace says. "At least we *have* boobs. Have you seen Alissa in the locker room? Everyone thinks she is *so* perfect, but without her clothes on, her boobs look like fried eggs—sunny-side up!"

"Remind me in the morning to tell Mama no eggs for breakfast," I say, then I flip over on my tummy and move in close to Grace. Even though everybody else in the house is asleep, I drop my voice to a whisper. "You never told me what happened with Tobey the other night."

"You mean did I let him touch my boobs?" she says, purposefully above a whisper. Sometimes she just loves to shock people. I think Mama wonders if she really is the best influence on me, but Mama is smart enough to realize she could never break up this friendship.

"Well, did you?" I say.

"Of course."

"Was it . . . nice?"

"It was *dee-licious*."

I close my eyes. "That's what I thought."

Everything I know about the birds and the bees I learned from Grace. She has this whole other life when we aren't together that is a mystery to me. Like she has a secret identity as a woman when she's not being a girl with me. I'm glad because I wouldn't have any other way of finding out about these things without Grace. Mama would certainly never talk to me about it, not that I would really want her to.

My whole life I've never seen her kiss Daddy any other way besides a quick peck on the cheek. I've never seen any *heat* between them. Not that I'd want them to make out in front of me or anything, I'm just kind of surprised I've never caught them doing anything or even heard them messing around in the room next to mine. Sometimes I wonder if they still do it at all. I know Daddy just goes to church to please Mama. I don't think he really believes in any of it. I think if it weren't for Mama, Daddy would probably lead a much different life.

Outside of my bedroom window on the other side of Grace I can hear the distant croaking of horny frogs. When I have a husband, I'm gonna kiss him properly, even in front of our children. And I won't pull away when he circles his arms around my waist from behind.

Grace flips over on her tummy like me, her face inches from mine, her chin resting on her folded hands. "Why don't I tell Trent you kinda like him?"

Trent is the Cats' star quarterback, out of my reach. I think about his curly black hair, broad shoulders and thick hands. "Maybe," I say, as I wonder what it would feel like to be touched by those hands.

Grace says, "Remember that time your mom took us shopping in Atlanta and after she split off to do her own thing, you and I took turns pretending to be blind, then deaf, in each store we went into?"

"That was so much fun. Kind of mean, but fun," I say. "I can't believe all those people actually believed us!"

"You were better at being blind," Grace says, "with that blank stare you can get going. You know people are watching you, but it doesn't even faze you."

"You were great at being deaf," I say. "The way you pretended to read my lips and flopped your hands around all wild-like—as if you know sign language!"

"That's me, Moon Turkey of the Wild Hands!" she says, then she begins to holler out a pretend-Indian chant as her hand quick-claps over her mouth.

I wiggle my toes and laugh at Grace. This is what Mama needs—a friend like I have. Not one of the old biddies to gossip with, but someone her own age, a real pal. Someone who can remind her how much fun life can be.

CHAPTER 4

I rub my eyes and look at the alarm clock on my night-stand—7:00 a.m. Daddy's snoring like a freight train in the next room. I sneak out of bed, leaving Grace sleeping there like the dead, and tiptoe down the hall toward the bathroom. I pause at Mama and Daddy's door to listen. I worry when he does that snort and sputter thing, like he forgets to breathe. But when I put my ear to the door, he's already awake.

"May?" he says. "Honey, why don't you come back to bed for a few minutes?"

"I just put my face on," she says. She must be sitting at her vanity table. "Besides," she says, "I think I hear Ruth Ann, and I need to get moving. No sense in wasting a perfectly good morning."

"That's exactly what I was thinking," Daddy says. The door swings opens as he's trailing off.

"Trixie!" Mama says. She gives me her wide lipsticked smile. She still has her floral housecoat on, but her face is perfect. Mama always says a lady never allows herself to be seen without her lipstick. "What sounds good for breakfast?" she says with enough energy to make you think she's been awake for hours.

I finish in the bathroom by splashing water on my face. That's my beauty routine. I go back to my room to check on Grace, but she's still sleeping. Daddy must have gone back to sleep, too, so I tiptoe back down the hall and into the kitchen. Ruth Ann is sitting on the stool watching Mama crack eggs.

"Can I have grape jelly with my biscuits?" Ruth Ann says.

"Of course you can, my little peach. You can have anything you want," Mama says without looking up.

"Hi, Trixie," Ruth Ann says. She's always happy to see me.

"Ruth Ann," Mama says. "Why don't you go outside and play for a few minutes while I finish up breakfast? In a few hours it'll be so hot you'll melt into a little puddle."

"Okay, Mama," she says.

I lift her down from the stool. "Stay in the yard," I say, opening the back door for her. She skips under my arm and out the door, barefoot and dressed in a pink bubble. She's getting a little old for those one-piece, poufy outfits Mama loves so much. Her pale, long legs look even scrawnier with nothing but elastic around her upper thighs.

Through the screen door I watch her trail a teensy green tree frog as it hops across the grass. That kid loves all of God's creatures. I walk over to the counter where Mama is rolling out the dough for biscuits.

Then, out of the early morning silence, comes a loud screech that seems to last for a full minute. I look at Mama and she looks at me. Her rolling pin is suspended in mid air. A car door is opening and shutting. We know it has just skidded to a stop in front of our house. "Ruth Ann?" I croak. But before either one of us can move, Daddy is running past us to the parlor and out the front door. He heard it too.

CHAPTER 5

After what could have happened to Ruth Ann with that *crazy out-of-town driver*, as Mama called him, I know I should be more careful on the road, but I still can't focus. I'm driving Daddy's pick-up without thinking about what I'm doing. The man's car probably didn't even get that close to Ruth Ann. When we got out there she was perfectly fine. Adults are always overreacting. Especially Mama.

"Praise Jesus for saving my baby," Mama wailed as she sat on the pavement and clutched Ruth Ann. You'd think she'd witnessed a miracle, like Ruth Ann had just walked on water. Daddy just stood there staring, unblinking, with his hands hanging on either side of him. The man, who had gotten out of his car and knelt down next to Ruth Ann and Mama, kept apologizing over and over, for what *could* have happened. It was kind of embarrassing.

In fact, Mama carried on all morning long. I really needed to get out of there, but I bided my time. Cooking lunch settled Mama down a bit, so by mid-afternoon I asked Daddy if I could take a drive in his truck.

What if I wrecked this truck right now? What would Mama do if I really was in an accident? Would she and Daddy finally hold each other and gaze lovingly at me as I lay in recovery from emergency surgery? Or as I lay in a coffin? "We almost forgot how precious *this* one is," they'd say.

I don't even know where I'm going, but I'm outside of town now, so I go ahead and turn down the road that leads to the state park. It's one of my favorite places to hang out in the summer—so remote there's hardly ever a tourist. And most of the locals are inside with their air conditioning this time of year.

I shut the rusty door of the truck and start on the zigzag path that leads down the cliff to the rushing water. When I get to the bottom, I step across some stones to my favorite big rock where I know I can think clearer. I sit there hugging my knees.

What if Ruth Ann had been hit by that car? I feel a little guilty for even imagining it, but out here alone I allow myself to wonder. In the shade of the ravine, it all starts spinning out like a movie in my mind.

Me sitting in the emergency room by Ruth Ann's body. Mama standing on the other side. Daddy just outside the room talking to the doctors, asking them questions, like if he can just get the details right, he'll have this solved, fixed, back the way it was.

Of course Mama wouldn't wanna leave Ruth Ann, and I wouldn't wanna leave Mama. Folded in two over the gurney, her tear-streaked face laying on the mattress next to Ruth Ann's, her puffy eyes closed, Mama would be unaware that I'm even in the room. The tears I've been blocking for Mama's sake would silently flow. They'd flow for Ruth Ann, my plucked-too-soon Buttercup. They'd flow for myself for having to feel this much pain. They'd flow for Mama, who will never be the same. Mama always says the Lord won't give you more than you can bear, but I know she wouldn't be able to bear this.

Then there'd be the funeral.

Me sitting there for two days in that stuffy funeral parlor while people come and tsk tsk about what a horrible waste it is. Such a beautiful, perfect little child and all. *Yes, she was beautiful*, I'd want to yell at them, *and I am just average.*

Like Mama, most of the old biddies from church—who'd show up in their dusted-off special-occasion hats—would look right through me, as though I'm not even there. They'd stand in a circle and in not-so-hushed voices question whether a three-year-old should have been allowed to play outside unsupervised. Then, switching from judgment to sympathy, "Bless her poor little heart," they'd say about Mama. Like me, they'd suspect Mama will never be the same, but I don't like hearing it come from them. They'd finally stop over and hug me, but their eyes would be on Mama. And their eyes would notice that Mama and Daddy aren't standing beside each other. Not the whole time.

The only one of the biddies who'd even speak to me is Miss Bertie. "It was God's will, Honey," she'd say, gripping my arm with her bony, dried-up fingers.

I'd keep myself from jerking away, which is what I'd really want to do. Maybe I'd tell her God's will is for me to knock her across the room. I'd never really hit her. One punch would probably land her on the floor where she'd break a hip or something. That's what everyone's always afraid old people are gonna do, break their hip. Like that's the worst thing that could ever happen.

"It's bad enough losing a sister," I'd say to Miss Bertie,

"but Mama and Daddy have lost a child, and that's way worse."

"You *are* a brave one, aren't you?"

"At least Ruth Ann didn't have to suffer," I'd say, unable to stop now. "The doctors all agreed she died on impact. She must have chased that frog all the way around the house and then into the street without realizing where she was—that's the only way she would have disobeyed Mama's rule to stay in the yard."

"The poor thing," Miss Bertie would say, now in tears. I'd make fun of her with Grace later.

"If I hadn't had my friend over to spend the night," I'd say to Miss Bertie, "I would have been up earlier that morning. Maybe Ruth Ann would have been hanging out with me—a lot of times we watch cartoons together on Saturday mornings—or maybe I would have gone outside with her."

"Don't blame yourself, child," she'd say.

From my rock, I kick off one sandal and dip my toes in the cool stream. Daddy always says I have a "flair for the dramatic," but it'd be Mama who'd go crazy with the *what ifs.*

She wouldn't be able to stop replaying that morning in her mind. She'd blame herself for sending Ruth Ann outside to play. And she'd blame Daddy. If he'd helped her out more, had taken more of an interest in the child raising, if he hadn't been lying around in bed that morning . . . . Daddy would try to tell her it's nobody's fault, and why does she always have to assign blame.

Later I'd hear them arguing in their bedroom next to mine. First a low murmur, then their voices would start to get loud, then they'd change to a desperate whisper-shout, then there'd be silence. The silence is always the scariest part. It means they've given up trying to understand each other.

In the weeks ahead, I'd try to move on with my life.

"I'm going out," I'd say as I walk past Mama. I'd look back, to see if she even notices me, but she'd be sitting in that fancy, straight-backed chair in the parlor, staring at nothing, her expressionless face turned slightly to the right.

When not in that chair, she'd be lying in Ruth Ann's bed, smelling the sheets she can't bring herself to wash. She'd stare up at the stars on Ruth Ann's ceiling. The plastic ones I tacked up there for her so at night in her bed she could feel like she's outside looking up at the sky. That kid loved being outside. Mama would be looking for Ruth Ann in those stars.

Mama would stay away from me. Just looking at me would remind her of her first thought when she knew she'd lost Ruth Ann—*Why not this one instead*? Oh, she wouldn't admit that out loud. She wouldn't even really admit it to herself. She can't handle going to that dark place in her heart where mothers think they'll never have to go. But I'd know the truth.

And then there's Daddy. He'd be back to work, back to driving his truck. Gone for a couple of days at a time. The silence between him and Mama would grow like a weed, vines thickening until they can't see each other anymore. The vines would grow around our whole house, too. Like in Ruth Ann's favorite movie *Sleeping Beauty*. If I believed in fairies, I would want them to put a spell on us so we could sleep until Ruth Ann wakes up. But I know there's no such thing as fairies. There's only God. And God would have let Ruth Ann die.

Mama wouldn't be able to bring herself to pray or be in

church anymore. Thinking about God would remind her that maybe she clung to Ruth Ann too tightly. The Bible says God is a jealous God and doesn't want us to worship any idols or persons before Him—maybe He knew Mama loved Ruth Ann better than Him. Maybe this is her punishment.

Can God see me now, sitting here on this slippery rock? Mama says He can see you all the time, no matter where you go. There's no hiding from God. Did He see my daydream? Does He know my terrible thoughts?

The croaking back and forth of frogs courting snaps me out of my trance. Suddenly I realize it's getting dark fast. The sound of the water lapping around the rocks must have lulled me half asleep. Sitting here alone I feel calmer than I've felt in a long time. If Ruth Ann had died that day, this is how I'd want to think of her—somewhere amidst the mountain's greenery and the water's white foam, at peace with the natural world and the spiritual one that are somehow tied together out here.

I hop off the rock and stone-jump my way back to the shore. As I start back up the path, it occurs to me that until now I hadn't thought about how dark it would be down here at night with no streetlights. I can't see a thing.

I let out a little giggle. "This is a fine mess you've gotten yourself in," I say out loud. "You've been here a thousand times. Just make your way up this path from memory."

I'm chanting, "Left. Left. Left, Right, Left," and marching forward like in the military drill when I hear, and feel, something whiz across the path directly in front of me and land hard on the other side. I stop in my tracks. I hear the deep "Ru-u-u-um" of a bullfrog. Bullfrogs are the biggest of all the frogs. Ruth Ann's little tree frog was only a couple of inches long. Bullfrogs can get up to nearly a foot.

"Whoa there, Froggy. This is a one-way street," I say into the darkness, relieved that it's just a harmless animal. But when I start marching again, another frog whizzes in front of me. Then comes the "Ru-u-u-um." I stop, then start. Another one. "Ru-u-u-um." Stop. Start. Another. Stop. They're jumping and landing all around me. My heart is beating fast now. I know I outweigh bullfrogs by a lot, but I'm blind right now. I'm rattled and unsure of what to do next.

"Calm down," I tell myself out loud. Should I just take off running to get this over with? But I don't want to step on one of them. I'm wearing sandals. I couldn't bear a squishy sound in the dark, then feeling blood and guts all over my toes. I wonder how high they're jumping. I don't want to walk right into one and feel its slimy skin against my bare chest or arms. Or worse yet, I don't want to feel one ricochet off my face.

"Ru-u-u-um," I hear echoing in every direction. It sounds like there's hundreds. What do these things do, all come out for a party as soon as it gets dark? Even though I can't see a thing anyway, I keep my eyes shut tight. Crossing my fingers, I start screaming and running at the same time. No one will hear my screams out here. I'm not even trying to call for help. I guess I'm hoping the screaming will scare the frogs a little, let them know they better get out of my way. Let them know I'm someone to be reckoned with.

As soon as I've worn out each scream, I take a quick, deep breath and let out a fresh one. I scream and run, pausing only long enough to decide whether I should zig or zag. It seems like this has been going on for an hour when I finally reach the top of the cliff and Daddy's truck. I open the door and fall in, slamming the door behind me to shut the frogs out. I rest my head on the steering wheel and pant, trying to catch my breath and quiet my pounding heart so I can drive home.

"Trixie one, frogs zero," I say, then I start laughing until tears are streaming down my face, and I don't know if I'm still laughing or if I'm crying.

###

Dawn White grew up in McMinnville, Tennessee before moving to Michigan where she worked and raised her family in the Ann Arbor area. Dawn was a college-level writing instructor for sixteen years, and then transitioned to roles in business development, marketing, and copy writing for software companies.

These days Dawn can usually be found at her cottage on the Collins River near Rock Island State Park in Tennessee, where she spent much of her childhood. She now enjoys spending time in nature with her husband, Rob, her children, Emma and Jake, and her Boxers, LuLu and Belle.

CPSIA information can be obtained
at www.ICGtesting.com
Printed in the USA
LVHW050354291220
675195LV00010B/337